# Wildflowers
## of the Midwest

*Adventure Quick Guides*

YOUR WAY TO EASILY IDENTIFY WILDFLOWERS

# Adventure Quick Guides

Organized by color for quick and easy identification, this Midwest guide is designed to help the curious nature seeker identify 153 species of the most common wildflowers found in the states of Illinois, Indiana, Iowa, Kansas, Kentucky, Michigan, Minnesota, Missouri, Nebraska, North Dakota, Ohio, South Dakota and Wisconsin. It features full-color images of wildflowers in bloom and icons showing how the leaves attach to the stems.

## MIDWEST WILDFLOWER FIELD GUIDES

For more information about wildflowers, such as the season of bloom, habitat, fruit and interesting gee-whiz facts, use Stan's field guides for these Midwest states:

## WILDFLOWERS OF THE MIDWEST PLAYING CARDS

Improve your wildflower identification skills with these beautiful cards by Stan Tekiela.

## STAN TEKIELA

Stan Tekiela is an award-winning photographer, naturalist and author of over 190 field guides, nature books, children's books and more about birds, mammals, reptiles, amphibians, trees and wildflowers.

Cover image by Stan Tekiela: Wood Lily
All images copyrighted. All images by Stan Tekiela unless otherwise noted:
Rick and Nora Bowers (Mayapple, Turtlehead), Jaret C. Daniels (Jacob's Ladder, Common Teasel, Spring Larkspur, Showy Orchis, Perfoliate Bellwort, Indian Paintbrush), Dudley Edmondson (Forget-me-not, Virginia Bluebells, False Indigo, Red Trillium, Nodding Trillium), Richard Haug (Star-flowered Solomon's Seal) and Connie Toops (Pokeweed), and English Plantain via Shutterstock.

Cover and book design by Lora Westberg
Edited by Sandy Livoti

10 9 8 7 6 5
**Wildflowers of the Midwest Quick Guide**
Copyright © 2017 by Stan Tekiela
ISBN 978-1-59193-703-6

Published by Adventure Publications
An imprint of AdventureKEEN
310 Garfield Street South
Cambridge, Minnesota 55008
(800) 678-7006
www.adventurepublications.net
All rights reserved
Printed in China

# How to Use This Guide

## KEY

- Wildflowers are sorted into nine groups by color and organized from smaller to larger. Leaf attachment icons are shown next to each wildflower. Descriptions include sizes and other important facts, such as cluster shape, number of petals or center color, to help you quickly identify the species.

- Plants marked with the N icon are considered noxious, detrimental to agriculture, the environment, people or recreation, by at least one state in the region. Each state has its own lists of problematic plants; familiarize yourself with your state's list so you can stay up to date.

## IDENTIFYING WILDFLOWERS

Within each color section, the wildflowers are arranged by the size of the flower, or the flower cluster, from small to large. Sometimes flowers are made up of many individual flowers in clusters that are perceived to be one larger flower. Therefore, these are ordered by the size of the cluster, not the individual flower. Clusters can be round, flat or spiked.

Within each of the nine color groups, flower color can vary. For example, a blue wildflower may look more like lavender, and a white flower may appear pinkish. Other wildflowers occur in a variety of colors. Keep this in mind when you are identifying a flower that fits the description but shows a color variance.

Wildflower leaves attach to stems in different ways. The leaf icons next to the flowers show alternate, opposite, whorl, perfoliate, clasping and basal attachments. Some wildflower plants have two or more types of leaf attachments.

 **ALTERNATE** leaves attach in an alternating pattern.

 **OPPOSITE** leaves attach directly opposite each other.

 **WHORL** leaves have three or more leaves that attach around the stem at the same point.

 **PERFOLIATE** leaves are stalkless and have a leaf base that entirely surrounds the main stem.

 **CLASPING** leaves are stalkless and have a leaf base that partly surrounds the main stem.

 **BASAL** leaves originate at the base of the plant and are usually grouped in pairs or in a rosette.

**Forget-me-not**
¼" wide baby blue flowers, each with 5 petals and a yellow center

**Narrowleaf Blue-eyed Grass**
½" wide blue flowers, 6 petals and a bright yellow center

**Asiatic Dayflower**
½" wide blue and white flowers, 2 blue upper petals and 1 white lower petal

**Round-lobed Hepatica**
½–1" wide pale blue-to-lavender flower on a single hairy stalk

**Sharp-lobed Hepatica**
½–1" wide flowers, 5–9 petals, blue to white, sometimes pink

**Jacob's Ladder**
½–1" long blue bell flowers in a spike cluster

**Virginia Bluebells**
clusters of bell-shaped flowers, 1" long, each with 5 fused petals forming a long tube

**Common Blue Violet**
1" blue-to-lavender or sometimes white flowers with 5 petals, on a single stem

# Mostly blue

## Chicory
sky-blue stalkless flowers, 1¼" wide, with as many as 20 square-tipped petals

## Bottle Gentian
1–1½" long tube flowers in clusters, each flower has 5 petals, closed tops

## Virginia Waterleaf
1–1½" round cluster, ¼–½" light blue flowers, 5 petals fuse to form a bell

## Alfalfa
1–2" spike cluster, each flower ¼–⅜" long, 1 large upper petal and 3 smaller lower petals

## Heal-All
1–2" spike cluster, ½" long violet blue flowers, upper petal forms a hood

## Pasqueflower
1–2" wide blue-to-white flowers, 5–7 petal-like sepals surround a yellow center

## Spiderwort
1–2" wide flowers, up to 10 per cluster, 3 blue-to-purple petals and yellow centers

## Bird's-foot Violet
1½" wide blue flower, 5 distinct petals with lower petals wider than the upper

**Lead Plant**
1–3" tight spike cluster, ⅛" long individual flowers with orange centers, 1–3' tall shrub

**Giant Blue Hyssop**
1–3" spike cluster of ¼" long tube flowers, tightly packed

**Common Teasel**
1–3" cluster, round to egg-shaped, made up of individual tube flowers, each ½" long

**Wild Blue Phlox**
2–3" flat cluster, 1" wide pale blue flowers, each made up of 5 petals

**Spring Larkspur**
2–4" open spike of 1–1½" long pea-like flowers, upper petals are longer and bend back

**Wild Lupine**
3–7" spike cluster of ⅝" wide blue-to-white pea-like flowers, 5 petals look like 3

**Pickerelweed**
4–6" spike clusters, blue flowers with 3 upper petals and 2 small dots on 3 lower petals

**False Indigo**
up to 10" spike, ½–1" long pea-like flowers alternate nearly perpendicular to the stem

# Mostly purple

## Four-o'clock
cluster of purple-to-pink flowers, ⅜" wide, 5 notched petals

## Dame's Rocket
purple, blue or white flowers, ½–1" wide, 4 round petals

## Spotted Knapweed
25–100 clusters of 1" wide lavender-to-purple flowers, sometimes white to red

## Shooting Star
single stalk with 1–5 nodding purple flowers, each 1" wide

## Showy Orchis
single stem with several 1" tall two-toned flowers, purple hood and white lower petals

## New England Aster
many bright purple and yellow flowers, 1–2" wide, sticky hairs cover the stalks

## Purple Prairie Clover
1–2" spike cluster of ⅛" long flowers with 5 petals

## Wild Bergamot
1–2" round cluster, ¼" long flowers each have a curved lower petal and a straight upper petal

### Wild Geranium
groups of delicate, pale lavender flowers, each flower 1–2" wide with 5 heavily veined petals

### Bull Thistle
reddish purple flower, 1½–2" wide, on a wide spiky base

### Field Thistle
2" wide pale purple flower head with a large, spiny green base

### Hoary Vervain
2–5" spike cluster, purple-to-blue tube-like flowers, ½" long, each have 5 fused petals

### Purple Coneflower
14–20 droopy purple-to-blue petals, 3–5" wide, surround the center cone

### Purple Fringed Orchid
6–10" spike cluster, each flower ½–1" wide, fine notches on petals form a fringe

### Rough Blazing Star
6–12" spike cluster, each flower round, ¾" wide, many flowers along the stem

### Purple Loosestrife
1–2' spike cluster of ½–¾" wide flowers tightly packed together

# Mostly yellow

**Yellow Wood Sorrel**
1 to many bright yellow flowers, ½" wide, made up of 5 petals

**Birds-foot Trefoil**
many bright yellow pea-like flowers, ½" long

**Perfoliate Bellwort**
shriveled-looking bell flower, 1" long, hangs down from a thin drooping stem, 6 petals

**Yellow Trout Lily**
1" wide yellow flower on a single stalk, 6 backward-curving petals

**Jewelweed**
1" long yellow tube flower with a sprinkling of dark reddish brown spots deep within

**Common St. Johnswort**
open cluster of up to 20 bright flowers, 1" wide, 5 yellow petals with black dots along the edges

**Gumweed**
upwards of 20 flowers, 1" wide, each with 20 or more short petals around a yellow center

**Marsh Marigold**
many bold yellow flowers, 1–1½" wide, with 5–9 petals

# Mostly yellow

**Common Dandelion**
single yellow flower, 1½" wide,
on a single stem

**Thin-leaved Coneflower**
upwards of 50 flowers, 1–2"
wide, each with 6–10 petals
surrounding a cone center

**Sneezeweed**
upwards of 100 flowers, 1–2"
wide, each with 10–15 wedge-
shaped petals and a ball center

**Large-flowered Bellwort**
droopy, shriveled-looking yellow
flower, 1–2" long, with 6 petals

**Wood Betony**
1–3" spike cluster of 2-lipped
flowers, each ¾" long, upper lip
arched, lower lip shorter

**Gray-headed Coneflower**
10–15 droopy petals surround a
cone, 2–2½" tall, 10–25 flowers
per plant, on single stalks

**Goat's Beard**
large dandelion-like flower,
2–2½" wide, on a stalk swollen
just below the flower

**Black-eyed Susan**
large yellow flower, 2–3" wide,
with 10–20 petals and a dark,
button-like center

# Mostly yellow

**Green-headed Coneflower**
25–50 flowers, 2–3" wide, each with 8–10 drooping yellow petals surrounding a green center

**Prickly Pear**
2–3" wide cactus flower with many yellow petals on fleshy, flat, broad pads (leaves) with spines

**Yellow Lady's Slipper**
2–3" tall with 1 flower per stalk, 4 brownish petals surround an inflated yellow petal

**Leafy Spurge**
2–3" flat cluster, 2 leaf-like "petals" (bracts) surround a tiny green flower, ⅛" wide

**Wild Parsnip**
many large 2–3" flat clusters of many tiny ¼" wide flowers

**Hoary Puccoon**
2–3" flat cluster, each yellow-to-orange flower, ½" wide, has 5 petals that form a small tube

**Winter Cress**
several 2–3" spike clusters of ¼" wide flowers, each with 4 petals that form a cross

**Woodland Sunflower**
up to 10 or more 2–4" wide yellow flowers, 10–17 petals surround a yellow center

# Mostly yellow

**Compass Plant**
several 3" wide yellow flowers on a tall stem, 25 petals

**Yellow Flag Iris**
1 to several large yellow flowers, 2½–4" wide, 6 petals, 3 larger and 3 smaller

**Cup Plant**
branched stalk with up to 30 flowers, 3–4" wide, 24–30 petals with a green-to-yellow center

**Stiff Goldenrod**
3–4" flat cluster of many tiny individual flowers, ⅜" wide, each with 7–10 petals

**Yellow Water Lily**
floating, cup-shaped flowers, 3–5" wide, with 4 large yellow (sometimes green) petals

**Common Sunflower**
sunny yellow flowers, 3–6" wide, 15–20 petals surround a large dark brown or purple center

**Butter-and-eggs**
3–6" spike cluster, 1" tall pea-like yellow and orange flowers, each with 5 fused petals

**Canada Goldenrod**
large 3–9" spike cluster, ¼" wide flowers on an arching stem

# Mostly yellow

### Yellow Sweet Clover
many thin spike clusters, 8" tall, with ¼" long pea-like flowers

### Evening Primrose
many 6–10" round clusters, each flower 1–2" tall with 4 petals and an X-shaped stigma

### American Lotus
very large flower, 6-10" wide, with pale yellow-to-white petals and a yellow center, stands up to 12" above the water's surface

### Common Mullein
very tall 1–2' spike cluster of ¾–1" wide flowers, each with 5 petals

# Mostly green

### Aborted Buttercup
tiny cone-shaped green flower, ¼" long, with 5 extremely tiny yellow petals

### Pineapple-weed
¼" green-to-yellow flowers, round to dome-shaped

# Mostly green

## Smooth Solomon's Seal
½–1" long bell flowers hang on short stalks from the main stem, 6 petals

## Blue Cohosh
2" round cluster of ½" wide flowers, 6 pointed petal-like sepals and 6 round petals

## Jack-in-the-pulpit
2–3" club-like spike cluster hidden within a green or purplish hood (pulpit) known as a spathe

## Ragweed
thin spike cluster, 1–5" long, of tiny green flowers, ⅛" wide

# Mostly brown

## Wild Ginger
1–2" long tube flower, brown to red with 3 pointed lobes, found at ground level

## Skunk Cabbage
3–6" spike cluster inside a large, brown-to-purplish, shell-like covering (spathe)

### Orange Hawkweed
¾–1" wide flowers clustered on a stem, made of 20–30 daisy-like petals known as ray flowers

### Spotted Touch-me-not
1" long orange tube flower with red spots, open mouth leads to a long, thin, sharply curved tube

### Michigan Lily
large orange-to-yellow flowers, 2–3" wide, with 6 petals that curve backward

### Turk's-cap Lily
large orange-to-yellow flowers, 2–3" wide, hang down and have 6 backward-curving petals

### Wood Lily
showy 2–3" wide orange flowers with brown spots stand upright at the end of a stalk

### Butterfly-weed
2–3" flat cluster of ⅜" wide individual flowers

# Mostly red

### Prairie Smoke
groups of 3–6 drooping bell flowers, each ¾" long flower has 5 pointy, petal-like sepals

### Indian Paintbrush
inconspicuous greenish flowers among a cluster of 1" long red-tipped "petals" (bracts)

### Red Clover
1" round cluster of ⅛–¼" long individual red flowers

### Columbine
group of 5 upside down red-to-orange tubes form a 1–2" long bell flower

### Red Trillium
single dull red-to-maroon flower, 1–2" wide, with 3 petals and 3 green sepals, on a stalk

### Swamp Milkweed
several 2–3" flat clusters, each flower ¼" wide, 5 downward petals and 5 upward petals

### Cardinal Flower
open spike cluster, 1–2' tall, with 1½" wide flowers alternating on the stem, 5 petals

# Mostly pink

**Spreading Dogbane**
groups of up to 10 bell flowers, each flower ⅜" long, 5 petals fuse to form a tube

**Crown Vetch**
1" round cluster of pea-like pink and white flowers, ¼–½" wide, 1–2' tall climbing vine

**Large-flowered Beardtongue**
open spike of 1–2" long tube flowers, petal tips roll backward

**Common Milkweed**
2" round cluster of ½" wide pink-tinged flowers with 5 downward-pointing petals

**Showy Lady's Slipper**
2–3" tall, 3 white pointed upper petals, 1 larger inflated pink and white lower petal

**Hedge Nettle**
2–3" spike cluster of ½–1" wide flowers, each with a pink upper hood and 3 lobed petals

**Motherwort**
3–6" spike cluster, individual flowers ⅜" long, spine-tipped

**Joe-pye Weed**
5–10" flat cluster, hundreds of ¼" wide individual flowers

# Mostly white

### Common Chickweed
¼" star-shaped flowers at the end of a tiny stalk, 5 deeply divided petals look like 10

### Daisy Fleabane
white and pink flowers with yellow centers, each flower ½" wide with up to 40 tiny petals

### Cut-leaved Toothwort
3–15 white-to-lavender flowers, ½" wide, each with 4 petals

### Rattlesnake Root
small white-to-cream and purple-tinged bell flowers, ½" long, hang down in clusters

### Spring Beauty
showy white-to-pink upright flowers, each ½–¾" wide

### Snow Trillium
single flower, ½–1" wide, above a whorl of leaves, 3 white petals and 3 green sepals

### Indian Pipe
1 waxy bell flower, ½–1" wide, per stem, very small scale-like leaves often go unnoticed

### Black Snakeroot
3–5 round clusters of tiny white-to-cream flowers, ½–1" wide

# Mostly white

**Dutchman's Breeches**
uniquely shaped waxy white flowers, ¾" long, several flowers on an arching stalk

**Wild Strawberry**
several white flowers, ¾" wide, each with 5 round petals and a yellow center

**English Plantain**
1" spike cluster with ⅛" tiny white flowers extending outward from the spike

**Hoary Alyssum**
1" spike cluster of tiny ¼" wide flowers, 4 notched petals look like 8

**Wild Calla**
large white petal wraps around a 1" tall, club-like cluster of tiny yellow flowers, ¼" wide

**White Clover**
1" round cluster on a single stalk, ¼" wide pea-like flowers

**Indian Hemp**
round cluster, 1" wide, made of 2–10 tiny whitish flowers, each ⅜" wide with 5 petals

**White Trout Lily**
1" wide bell flower hangs down from a single stem, 3 petals and 3 petal-like sepals

# Mostly white

**Wood Anemone**
single flower with 5 petals, 1" wide, rises above the leaves

**White Campion**
many 1" wide flowers with 5 deeply notched petals stand above a green bladder

**Nodding Trillium**
single white flower, 1–1½" wide, 3 white petals and 3 green sepals

**Yellow Gentian**
cluster of white closed tube flowers, each 1–1½" long

**White Snakeroot**
1–2" flat cluster made up of many tiny flowers, ⅛" wide

**Pennycress**
1–2" spike cluster of ¼" wide flowers, 4 white petals form a cross shape

**Bur Cucumber**
1–2" round cluster of ½" wide individual flowers, each with 5 petals, 2–10' tall climbing vine

**Field Bindweed**
1–2" wide tube flower with 5 petals fusing to form a funnel, 1–6' tall climbing vine

# Mostly white

## Ox-eye Daisy

white and yellow flower, 1–2" wide, on a single stalk, with up to 20 petals

## Mayapple

solitary hanging white flower, 1–2" wide, with 6–9 waxy petals

## Bloodroot

bright white 1½" wide flowers, each on a stalk, 8–10 long petals surround a yellow center

## White Prairie Clover

1–3" spike cluster of tiny flowers, ⅛" long, each with 5 petals

## Star-flowered Solomon's Seal

1–3" spike cluster of star-shaped creamy white flowers, ¼" wide

## Red Baneberry

dense 1–3" round cluster, ¼" wide flowers produce a cluster of shiny red poisonous berries

## White Baneberry

round to elongated cluster, 1–3" wide, ¼" wide flowers produce shiny white poisonous berries

## Garlic Mustard

1–3" round cluster of ¼" wide individual flowers, 4 petals

# Mostly white

### Cut-leaved Teasel
1–3" cluster, round to egg-shaped, made up of ½" long tube flowers

### Boneset
2–3" flat cluster, multiple tiny flowers, ¼" wide, pack together and look like one flower

### Turtlehead
2–3" spike cluster, 1–1½" long white tube flowers have 2 petals forming the tube

### Hedge Bindweed
2–3" long white-to-pink tube flowers, each with 5 petals, 3–10' tall climbing vine

### Water Hemlock
delicate 2–4" flat cluster made up of tiny flowers, ⅛" wide

### Common Yarrow
2–4" flat cluster, each flower ¼" wide, 4–6 (usually 5) white petals, sometimes pink

### Catnip
2–4" spike cluster, ½" long tube-like flowers made up of 2 large petals with purplish spots

### Virgin's Bower
2–4" round cluster of 1" wide flowers, each with 4–5 petals, 6–10' tall climbing vine

# Mostly white

### Large-flowered Trillium
single white-to-pink flower, 2–4" wide, 3 petals and 3 green sepals

### False Solomon's Seal
3–5" spike cluster at the end of an arching stem, tiny star-shaped flowers, ⅛" wide

### Queen Anne's Lace
3–5" flat cluster of ¼" wide white flowers, a single purple floret in the center of the cluster

### White Water Lily
large white floating flower, 3–6" wide, composed of many pointed petals around a yellow center

### Cow Parsnip
very large flat cluster, 4–8" wide, ½" wide white-to-purple flowers with notched petals

### Pokeweed
6–10" open spike cluster of ¼" wide white flowers, each with 5 petal-like sepals

### Flat-topped Aster
6–10" flat cluster, ½–¾" wide flowers with 10–15 petals and yellow centers

### Culver's Root
10–12" tall, thin spike cluster of tube flowers, ¼" long, 4 fused petals form the tube

*Adventure Quick Guides*

# Only Midwest Wildflowers
## Organized by color
for quick and easy identification

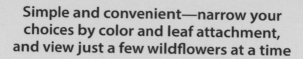

Simple and convenient—narrow your
choices by color and leaf attachment,
and view just a few wildflowers at a time

- Pocket-size format—easier than laminated foldouts
- Professional photos of flowers in bloom
- Sizes and leaf icons for comparison and identification
- Based on Stan Tekiela's best-selling wildflower field guides

Get these great *Adventure Quick Guides* for your area

ISBN 978-1-59193-703-6  **U.S. $9.95**

5 0 9 9 5

9 781591 937036

**Adventure** PUBLICATIONS
an imprint of Adventure**KEEN**

NATURE/WILDFLOWERS/MIDWEST